Great Lake Shoreline, by Hoyt Avery

Cover photo: Ice-coated limbs in the early morning, by Hoyt Avery

Come Explore

MICHIGAN THE BEAUTIFUL

Copyright 1986
First Edition 1986
Reprinted 1989

by Anita Avery, McCollum &
Avery Color Studios
Published by Avery Color Studios
Au Train, MI 49806
Library of Congress Card No. 86-81190
ISBN 0-932212-48-4

To Michael and Rebecca

Never stop looking for an adventure

Photo by Anita Avery McCollum

Michigan Sunrise, by Hoyt Avery

State Motto - If You Seek Pleasant Peninsulas,
Look About You.

The Beauty of Fall, by Hoyt Avery

Foreword

Children today must be thinking in universal terms in most all areas of life. Global education is mandate for all who participate in futures education. Yet, we all must have a foundation in where we are, our surroundings, and a value for our history.

This text is intended to give a parent or a teacher a visually stimulating, orderly arrangement of information, for Michigan children, of their surroundings. In addition, the photographs of each represent the history and beauty of the state. The organization and focus are designed to motivate children to know and, hopefully, value their home area. The material covers, at least partially, a void in social studies resources designed for young children.

There are many unique features aside from the history and geography. The selection of many geographic and historic spots were chosen to stimulate further study of areas that would be of interest to the reader's own specific life interests. Thus, the selections give the parent and teacher very many starting points for building additional search activities for the children. The reading levels have been tested and geared for growth and could be infused into the writing and reading activities of the middle primary grades. We feel this work will be a welcome addition for children's social studies.

Paul Kimball
Assistant Superintendent
Upper Peninsula Outreach Office
Michigan Department of Education

MICHIGAN THE BEAUTIFUL

by Dr. David B. Steinman

Michigan the Beautiful!
Paradise the red man knew,
Where the deer still range the greenwood
And the lakes reflect the blue.

Michigan the Beautiful!
Where the smoke of campfires curled,
Now a thousand wheels are humming
Day and night to serve the world.

Michigan the Beautiful!
Haven of the hearts desire;
Smiling farms and gleaming cities
Keep alive our Freedom's fire.

Michigan the Beautiful!
Land of forest, lake and stream,
Home of sturdy pioneers,
Builders of the Western Dream.

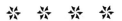

(This poem by Dr. David B. Steinman, designer of the world-famous Mackinac Bridge, was written for the 1959 observance of Michigan Week.)

And the lakes reflect the blue, by Hoyt Avery

The word *Michigan* came from various Native American words such as Michigama and Mishigamaw. They mean large lakes or great water. The word was used by the Indians when talking about Lake Michigan. It was many years before the word was used as a name for the entire area bordered by the Great Lakes.

Lake Huron Shoreline, photo by Hoyt Avery

Photo by Hoyt Avery

State Flower - Apple Blossom. This flower was chosen because it represented the perfumed beauty of Michigan's springtime.

State Bird - Robin. A well-known bird seen in the yards, orchards or woods all over Michigan. The adult bird is orange-breasted and has acquired the nickname of "Robin Red-breast". The Robin builds its nest of grass and mud in trees, shrubs or on buildings. They sing a series of six to ten whistled phrases of three or four notes.

Photo by Anita Avery McCollum

Photo by Hoyt Avery

State Tree - White Pine. This tree was honored by
the state because of its contribution to Michigan's
lumbering era and because it stands straight, tall,
proud, often alone and is symbolic of a strong state,
often leaders in the nation.

Photo Courtesy Travel Bureau, Michigan Dept. of Commerce

State Flag - adopted in 1911

Michigan's state flag is dark blue bearing a Coat of Arms. The phrases are Latin and say three different things. *"Tuebor"* means "I will defend", *"e pluribus unum"* means "From many, one", and the longest phrase is our state motto, *"Si quaeris peninsulam amoenam circumspice"*, or "If you seek a pleasant peninsula, look about you". This motto was written in 1835.

The flag of Michigan reminds us that in the past three hundred and fifty years the flags of France, England, and Spain have also flown over this land.

Photo Courtesy Travel Bureau, Michigan Dept. of Commerce

The Coat of Arms

Also known as Michigan's State Seal, the Coat of Arms was styled after the seal used by Hudson Bay Company. This large trading company was a business back in the early years of the Michigan Territory. It still is operating in Canada.

Michigan was admitted to the union in 1837 as the nation's 26th state. Before this region became the state of Michigan it was part of the land that made up the Northwest Territory. Later, it was re-divided and called the Michigan Territory, which included the present states of Michigan, Iowa, Minnesota, Wisconsin and part of the Dakotas. In 1805, when Michigan was still a territory, the city of Detroit was selected as the seat of government and a capitol building was built. It was a wooden structure sixty by ninety feet. Detroit remained the capital for ten years after Michigan's statehood.

In 1848 the capitol was relocated to Lansing. An extravagantly ornamented dome-top building was completed in 1879. It houses the two legislative chambers and the governor's office. Emblems representing Michigan's growth and development are found in many locations within the capitol. A large pediment shows a Native American woman throwing away her scalping knife and tomahawk in exchange for a globe and a book, symbolizing education and civilization; a female figure, sitting on a bale of merchandise, surrounded by a ship's anchor, a felled log, an axe and a pile of lumber, symbolizing industry; and a third figure, placed against a background of plowhandles and mining tools, signifying agriculture and mining. There are paintings in the classical Greek style in the dome. These paintings illustrate the progress of the state in art, agriculture, shipping, lawmaking and science. The halls of the capitol contain murals which tell various stories of Michigan.

Front Walk of the Capitol, Photo by Hoyt Avery

The Capitol Building in Lansing, Michigan

German Maypole found in Frankenmuth, photo by Hoyt Avery

Many towns in Michigan were founded by people from other countries. Some of these towns still celebrate their heritage with annual festivals; for example, Holland, which was settled by the people of the Netherlands and Frankenmuth, which was a German settlement.

Windmill in Holland, photo courtesy Travel Bureau, Michigan Dept. of Commerce

Lake Superior

St. Mary River

UPPER PENINSULA OF MICHIGAN

Lake Huron

Lake Michigan

LOWER PENINSULA OF MICHIGAN

St. Clair River

Lake Ontario

Lake Erie

Michigan is a large state made up of an Upper and Lower Peninsula. Its bordering states are Wisconsin, Ohio and Indiana.

The waters around the state are known as "The Great Lakes". They are Lake Superior, Lake Michigan, Lake Huron and Lake Erie. Lake Ontario is also a Great Lake, but its water does not border Michigan's shoreline. It is located farther east toward the state of New York. All the Great Lakes are fresh water unlike the salt water of the oceans. Lake Superior is the largest, the deepest and the coldest of all the five lakes.

Beautiful Swan, photo courtesy of Travel Bureau, Michigan Dept. of Commerce

Michiganders or Michiganians are proud of their clear water, fresh air, and deep forests. This is why Michigan is often a national leader in protecting its wildlife and natural resources.

It is said Michigan's greatest resource is its water. The Great Lakes with their connecting rivers, form the largest body of fresh water in the world. Besides the Great Lakes, Michigan has more than 11,000 inland lakes.

The Bobcat, photo courtesy the Department of Natural Resources

The Otter, photo courtesy the Department of Natural Resources

It is a fact that any place in the state of Michigan is within six miles of a lake or stream.

Ducks on a pond, photo by Hoyt Avery

Michigan has many nicknames: Water Wonderland, Winter Wonderland, The Land of Hiawatha, and The Great Lakes State. Another common nickname is The Wolverine State. The wolverine does not live in Michigan anymore and some historians question if it ever did. The reason Michigan is called The Wolverine State is believed to be because many of these animals lived in Canada and were trapped heavily. Their pelts were transported by the way of Mackinac to eastern markets lending belief to the term, The Wolverine State.

Highbanks of the Au Sable, photo by Hoyt Avery

Morning mist on Island Lake, photo by Hoyt Avery

The Mackinac Bridge, photo by Hoyt Avery

In 1957 the Upper and Lower Peninsula were joined at the Straits of Mackinac by the Mackinac Bridge. The bridge is five miles long and is the world's longest suspension bridge. The Mackinac Bridge is recognized by designers as America's most beautiful bridge.

Last trip for the car ferry, photo by Norton Avery

Before the bridge was built, everyone had to drive their cars onto a ferry boat in order to go across the water to St. Ignace or Mackinaw City. Now, because of the "Mac Bridge", people can visit the entire state more easily.

Fort Mackinac on Mackinac Island, photo by Hoyt Avery

Today ferryboats still go to Mackinac Island. No automobiles are permitted on the island and all travel is by horse and buggy, bicycle, or by foot. Historic Fort Mackinac still overlooks the harbor and town with its colorful gardens and quaint shops.

Because of the abundant water, resources are moved by ship, up and down the Great Lakes, over to large cities like Chicago, or down the St. Lawrence Seaway to the ocean. Big ships, called freighters, can be seen in many of the harbors of Michigan as they pass through the Soo Locks and travel the St. Clair River.

A "Salty" going through the Soo Locks, heading back to the ocean, photo by Hoyt Avery

Iron ore freighter going through the Soo Locks, photo by Hoyt Avery

Two other transportation marvels in Michigan are the mile-long Detroit-Windsor railway and car tunnel and the underwater tunnel at Port Huron. The Detroit-Windsor tunnel is the first auto traffic tube ever built between two nations. It is eighty feet below the surface of the Detroit River. Port Huron, Michigan, and Sarnia, Ontario, built the first electrified underwater railway tunnel in 1891, again joining two major cities and two countries.

Because of our northern location in the United States, Michigan has four beautiful and very distinct seasons.

Michigan's Four Seasons.

Winters are usually very cold and some areas in the state get over 200 inches of snow per year. The spring thaw generally begins in late March. The spring rains turn everything green and soon the wildflowers are in full bloom.

Winter Wonderland, photo by Hoyt Avery

The crisp colors of spring, photo by Hoyt Avery

Rampaging waterfalls, photo by Hoyt Avery

All the color of Fall, photo by Hoyt Avery

Summer is welcomed in mid-June with warm sunshine and temperatures. The changing color of the leaves and flocks of birds flying south in October announce the arrival of fall. The days grow shorter and temperatures cool. Winter will soon return.

Michigan's four seasons encourage a variety of outdoor sports. People enjoy hunting, fishing, skiing, boating, hiking, camping, and snow-mobiling.

Tourism is a growing industry in the state. Plentiful resorts, motels, campgrounds, recreational sites, and state and federal parks exist in Michigan to accommodate the traveler's needs. Whether visiting historic or scenic attractions, exploring waterfalls, skiing, or enjoying hunting or fishing - Michigan has it all.

The highway system in Michigan is known as one of the best in the nation. Michigan pioneered in creating safer roads, signs, signal lights and rest stops. Michigan claims the very first roadside park in the United States.

Beautiful Whitetail Deer, photo by Hoyt Avery

The fun of canoeing, photo by Hoyt Avery

Abundant wildlife, photo by Hoyt Avery

Great Lake Coho Salmon, photo by Hoyt Avery

Many people tour Michigan just to view and photograph her many waterfalls. There are more than 150 beautiful waterfalls in Michigan and almost all of them are in the Upper Peninsula.

Ocqueoc Falls, photo by Hoyt Avery

Tahquamenon Falls in Winter, photo by Hoyt Avery

Towering Munising Falls in Early Spring, photo by Hoyt Avery

Laughing Whitefish Falls, photo by Hoyt Avery

Quaint Scott Falls, photo by Hoyt Avery

**Michigan is a special place. It has three
beautiful National Parks or Lakeshores.**

Isle Royale National Park is an island, surrounded by a host of smaller islands, located far out in Lake Superior. In this wilderness area a hiker, backpacker, boater, or canoe enthusiast can explore the islands and see many interesting things: prehistoric copper mines, volcanic lava rock formations, unusual wildlife such as foxes, wolves, and moose, wildflowers, or fantastic scenery. The island is the only place in the world where the gemstone Greenstone is found. It is a lovely deep green stone with a turtle shell pattern. The Greenstone is Michigan's State Gemstone.

The backpacking, the adventure...Isle Royale, photo by Anita Avery McCollum

Sleeping Bear National Lakeshore is located in the Lower Peninsula, on Lake Michigan. The Sleeping Bear Sand Dunes are a scenic treasure of the world. The miles of dunes were formed during the Ice Age when glaciers pushed the sands into place. The hills and gorges are always different for the wind shifts them constantly, creating a never-ending attraction for thousands of visitors each summer.

Shifting sands of Sleeping Bear Dunes, photo by Hoyt Avery

The third national park, **Pictured Rocks National Lakeshore,** is located in the Upper Peninsula along the shore of Lake Superior. Visitors fish, camp, hike the shoreline trails, look at waterfalls and sand dunes or have fun walking the beach looking for pretty stones.

The picturesque Miner's Castle, photo by Hoyt Avery

Industry in Michigan

Michigan is an industrial state because of its location near the world's greatest supply of fresh water. The low cost of water transportation on the Great Lakes and the St. Lawrence Seaway makes Michigan goods available on world markets. Detroit is closer *by water* to such European nations as England, Sweden, and Belgium than New York City. The state is also close to major sources of raw materials, to large population areas for marketing, and has the highly skilled laborers needed for production. Access to electrical power and natural gas combined with outstanding research and technical centers provides a favorable industrial climate in Michigan. In addition, Michigan has excellent highways, railroads, and air services.

There are so many kinds of industry represented in Michigan but some of the most well known are auto, chemical, medicines, mining, cereal, baby food, paper, ship and boat building, furniture, cement and the never-ending high technology industry.

Michigan's Lower Peninsula is a center for manufacturing. Its greatest claim to fame is the "Motor City", Detroit, automotive capitol of the world, ranking among the largest cities in the nation. Detroit's industrial revolution of the early 1900's helped to develop other industrial cities like Battle Creek, Lansing, Kalamazoo, Flint, and Saginaw.

For generations Michigan mined many of its minerals such as gypsum, salt, calcium-magnesium chlorides, copper, bromine, iron ore, sand and gravel, petroleum, natural gas and coal, filling the needs of industry throughout the country.

Michigan is also an agricultural state. Farms around the countryside raise a wide variety of fruits and vegetables. Many farms have large herds of dairy cows which produce much of the nation's dairy products. Farmers celebrate their harvests annually with large festivals around the state. We stand among the leaders in the production of beans, cherries, potatoes, rhubarb, apples, grapes, blueberries, cucumbers, spearmint, strawberries, asparagus and plums.

Apple Orchard in bloom, photo by Hoyt Avery

Thousands of years ago great glaciers pushed their way down from the north, forming the Great Lakes. During this Ice Age, glaciers created Michigan's abundant water resources, mineral deposits, and left a rich fertile soil for farming. In the glacial deposits scientists found skeletons or fossil remains of shaggy-haired mammoths and mastodons, larger than elephants, which once roamed Michigan. Scientists also located skeletons of whales which had once lived in Michigan before the glaciers, proving that the water was here long before the land.

Volcanoes erupted, pouring out melted rock everywhere. Lava and evidence of the shifting of Michigan's rock can still be seen today in many parts of the state. They have created some of the most interesting rock formations in the United States.

Parts of skull and teeth of an American Mastodon found at the Shelton Mastodon Excavation Site, Oakland County, photo by J. Shoshani

Bare lava rock found on Isle Royale, photo by Hoyt Avery

History tells us that the natives of the Michigan area were Indians of several groups. By far the largest number of Michigan Indians belonged to the Algonquin group. Among the Algonquin nations were the Chippewa or Ojibway, the Potawatomi, the Ottawa, and the Miami. Related to the Iroquois nation were the Huron or Wyandot. The Fox and Mascouten nations, whose hunting grounds were in Wisconsin, were a part of the seige of Detroit in 1712.

Chippewa Native American dance,
photo by Hoyt Avery

Michigan still has four Native American reservations today where one can see the old dances and handmade craft, hear the songs and Indian legends retold. Many towns and counties in Michigan were named after words and names from the Indian language. Trails which they walked have become major highways.

Photo by Hoyt Avery

Chief Little Elk, of the Chippewa Indian tribe, photo by Hoyt Avery

The Great Lakes region was first discovered in 1534 by a French explorer named Jacques Cartier. He was searching for a water route to the Pacific Ocean and discovered the St. Lawrence River and Lake Superior. He believed it to be an arm of the great sea and possibly the Northwest Passage leading to India. The search for the Northwest Passage and the desire for animal fur continued to bring the French adventurers back to the New World and Michigan's Upper Peninsula.

Painting by Remington shows a friendly meeting of the Trapper and the Native American Indian, photo courtesy of Michigan State Archives

Follow the exploration of Cartier and Nicolet

No other section of the United States was fought over in history by the French and British more than Michigan. Each country wanted to control the fabulous wealth of the Great Lakes region and its valuable fur trade.

Almost 100 years later, around 1608, another explorer named Samuel de Champlain pushed his way up the St. Lawrence as far as Montreal and established a Trading Post. There he bartered with many Huron Indians who wore copper ornaments and traded beautiful copper wares. Through sign language he learned of another large lake, far north, called Lake Superior, and of the land of the copper which the Indians mined.

In 1634 the first real Christian mission was set up among the Huron Indians along the lakeshore bearing their name. It was in this year, one explorer and trader named Jean Nicolet, explored Lake Huron until he passed the Straits of Michili-mackinac (Straits of Mackinac) and entered Lake Michigan. He followed the northwest side of Lake Michigan's coast until he reached Green Bay. Later in 1668 Father Jacques Marquette established a mission at Sault Ste. Marie.

Even though the British controlled Michigan for only a short time they greatly influenced the state--- leaving the English language---English common law---many English customs---and much of the basic structure of the English government. Little French culture remains in Michigan today except for the names of some coastline cities, nine of the county names and the historic monuments in memory of Father Marquette, Cadillac, Nicolet and other famous figures who introduced European civilization to the Native American while the French held control over Michigan Territory.

Michigan has a lot of history to enjoy. Many forts, covered bridges, lighthouses, monuments, iron and copper mines, virgin pine forests, the capitol building and art and cultural centers exist here. It is a leader in education, a model in conservation, a pioneer in transportation progress and a land rich in folklore of American history.

Shrine of the Snowshoe Priest is located in L'Anse. Bishop Frederic Baraga moved about Michigan, Wisconsin, Minnesota and Canada for thirty-seven years, making God known and loved by all men. The shrine itself rises six stories above the Red Rock Bluffs between the villages of Baraga and L'Anse. It is made of brass and holds a seven foot cross and snowshoes twenty-six feet long.

The Shrine of Bishop Baraga, known as the Snowshoe Priest, photo by Hoyt Avery

Father Marquette Monument, erected in his memory in Marquette, Michigan, photo by Hoyt Avery

Mine shaft located in Michigan's Copper Country, photo by Hoyt Avery

Monument of Father Marquette.
Father Jacques Marquette was a favorite missionary working tirelessly among the Michigan Native Americans in the interest of Christianity. He was taken ill on one of his journeys and died on May 18, 1675 near Ludington. This monument in his honor is located in Marquette, Michigan.

Copper Mine. For generations Michigan has mined many of its minerals such as gypsum, salt, calcium-magnesium chlorides, copper, bromine, iron ore, sand and gravel, petroleum, natural gas and coal, filling the needs of industry throughout the country.

Lighthouse on Lake Huron. Lighthouses are an attraction to many people and historians. Many, around the coast of the Great Lakes, are being restored or preserved for people to see. With their restoration is coming a new awareness of maritime history and shipwrecks.

Fallasburg Covered Bridge. There are only four truly authentic covered bridges in the state and three of them are within 25 miles of each other. They are Whites, Fallasburg and Bradfield, located in the Grand Rapids area. The Langley Covered Bridge is located in Centreville and is the longest of the four, with three spans of ninety-four feet each. Each bridge cost about $2,000.00 to build back in the 1860's, 70's and 80's.

Port Sanilac Lighthouse on Lake Huron, photo by Hoyt Avery

Michigan's Fallasburg Bridge, photo by Hoyt Avery

A tribute to Michigan's lumbermen, photo by Hoyt Avery

View across the Lake of the Clouds, photo by Hoyt Avery

Lumberman's Monument is located on the Au Sable River. The words on it read, "Erected to perpetuate the memory of the pioneer lumbermen of Michigan through whose labors was made possible the development of the prairie states."

Lake of the Clouds is located along Lake Superior and in the Porcupine Mountains State Park. This breathtaking view from the mountains looks down on the Carp River and the largest stand of virgin timber in the state.

Historic Shrine in Muskegon honoring the "Man with the Branded Hand", photo by Hoyt Avery

The ghost town of Fayette, photo by Hoyt Avery

The Branded Hand Shrine was erected in honor of Captain Jonathan Walker. The "underground railroad" was started in 1832, by which slaves were helped to escape from bondage to Canada or other locations where they would find safety. Captain Walker was one of the assistants on this route. He was caught while helping seven slaves escape from their masters and convicted in 1844 by a Florida court as a slave stealer. As part of his sentence the letters "S.S." were branded in the palm of his right hand.

Fayette State Park is in the Upper Peninsula on Lake Michigan. White limestone cliffs surround the beautiful harbor ghost town. History of the Upper Peninsula mining industry and this once bustling smelter town are captured in a restored museum, old buildings and an interpretive center.

Beautiful Beaumont Tower, photo by Hoyt Avery

Fort Michilimackinac guarded the Straits in early Michigan history, photo by Hoyt Avery

Beaumont Tower is at Michigan State University in East Lansing. The University was the first agricultural college in the world. The college, founded in 1855, is the nation's first land-grant college and was originally known as Michigan Agricultural College.

Fort Michilimackinac and the Mackinac Bridge are located at Mackinaw City. It was controlled by both the French and the British in early Michigan history. This fort is open to the public and is great fun to see, with its many animated exhibits and historical displays.

Although Henry Ford did not invent the first automobile, he did create the first automobile manufacturing plant where a mass assembly line was used. The plant was located in Detroit. This invention started an industrial growth in Michigan never to be forgotten. Today there is beautiful Greenfield Village and Henry Ford Museum in the Detroit area which can take you for a stroll through history.

During World War II the automobile industries converted to production of war materials.

This photograph shows one of the first assembly line productions done by Ford Company in 1913, photo courtesy of Michigan State Archives

A Ford assembly line in 1932, photo courtesy of Michigan State Archives

Clock Shop at Greenfield Village, photo by Hoyt Avery

An interesting part of Michigan history is its logging days of the White Pine. At one time huge forests of White Pine, ideal for the lumber needed to build the cities of the nation, covered the north country. Loggers came into this wilderness and scalped the countryside of almost all its beautiful timber. Imagine the prairies of northern Michigan stretching to the far horizon, covered with nothing but stumps.

The Kingston Plains where once the big pine grew, photo by Hoyt Avery

Stumps reminding us of the past and new growth showing us the future, photo by Hoyt Avery

Of the original 36,494,000 acres of land in Michigan, 35,200,000 acres were timberland. Today, forestry programs manage the forests so there will always be the necessary timber for industry as well as the beautiful woodlands needed for wildlife and recreation. Michigan still ranks high among the Great Lakes states in timber and wood product industries.

In 1850 there were at least 800 sawmills in the state. Today, most of the forests are second and third generation trees which have reseeded themselves or have been planted to replace those original pine forests.

Besides the many pines, Michigan has forests of oak, hickory, ash, walnut, hemlock, maple, beech, poplar, and others. One researcher has found 85 varieties of trees growing in Michigan; more than in any other state, or more than can be found in all of Europe. Michigan produces 95% of the world supply of birds-eye maple.

MICHIGAN HAS

★ the biggest state east of the Mississippi in land and water area and the longest freshwater shoreline of any state in the union.

★ the first railway to be built in the United States west of the Allegheny Mountains... a 35 mile line between Toledo and Adrian. At the time Toledo was still a part of Michigan Territory.

★ the Detroit River, the busiest waterway in the world and the St. Mary's ship canal and the Soo Locks handle more cargo tonnage than any other of the world's leading canals.

★ Niles -- City of Four Flags -- the only spot in Michigan which has been under the rule of four nations in its history — France, Spain, Britain and finally the United States.

★ the Tahquamenon Falls in the Upper Peninsula is the famous "golden stream" of Longfellow's "Song of Hiawatha".

★ a globe location of 45th parallel. The state lies midway between the equator and the north pole.

★ the University of Michigan, the oldest state university in the country created directly by voters through their state constitution. It is known as the "Mother of State Universities" and is located in Ann Arbor.

★ the third oldest city in America. It is Sault Ste. Marie and was founded in 1668 by Father Jacques Marquette.

★ the first ski club in the United States organized at Marquette in 1863 and the National Ski Museum and Hall of Fame are located at Ishpeming.

★ the first commercial radio station in the country. WWJ began broadcasting in Detroit in 1922.

★ the Ontonagon boulder, the largest single piece of native copper in the world. It was discovered in 1667 and placed on display in the Smithsonian Institution in 1858.

A Few More Facts...

★ For 155 years the French governors in Canada ruled the territory which is now Michigan.

★ Michigan was inhabited by Native Americans long before Columbus discovered America in 1492.

★ Charles A. Lindbergh was raised in Detroit and in May of 1927 made the first nonstop flight by plane from New York to Paris.

★ The French spelling for the city of Detroit was De Troit back in the 1600's.

★ Thomas A. Edison invented the first electrode battery in Port Huron in 1861.

★ W.K. Kellogg and C.W. Post were the founders of America's cereal foods industry at Battle Creek.

★ Herbert H. Dow was a pioneer in creating the chemical industry and founded Dow Chemical Company.

★ Henry Ford's first company went bankrupt in 1899 but he began again and the Ford Motor Company revolutionized the automobile industry with the Model T.

★ Abraham Lincoln delivered his only speech in Michigan in Kalamazoo in 1856.

★ The American Red Cross offered its first disaster relief to victims of the devastating 1881 forest fires in Michigan's Thumb area.

★ Michigan's salt was discovered by state geologist Douglas Houghton in 1838 and now Michigan is the number one producer of salt in the United States.

★ Muskegon was the largest lumbering port in Michigan's west coast from the 1850s to the 1890s and was known as "the city that cut the lumber to build Chicago".

★ George Armstrong Custer who was killed in the Battle of the Little Big Horn in 1876 was born and raised in Monroe, Michigan.

★ A fur trader on Mackinac Island, Alexis St. Martin survived a gun shot wound to the abdomen to gain fame as "the man with the window in his stomach". Dr. William Beaumont first witnessed the digestive process through this window in 1822 and made medical history.

★ Singapore, located at the mouth of the Kalamazoo River in Allegan county was a busy lumber shipping port in the 19th century. Now it's a ghost town totally buried under sand dunes.

MICHIGAN IS—

A State of majestic beauty,---
God made it so---He intended it
for man's use and enjoyment.---
Land,-lots of it---for crops
and pastures---Forests for beauty,
utility and wildlife,---Marshes
for waterfowl,---cat tails and
pussywillows.---
Mountains and rolling hills---
Fertile valleys for meandering streams.
Water,-enough for industry, health and
recreation.---
If you have eyes to see, --- and ears
to hear,---You too, will love
MICHIGAN.

by Norton Louis Avery 1964

Countrysides in Michigan

Canada Geese

Blue Water Bridge at Port Huron crossing
the St. Clair River

Old steam engine in Cadillac

Old feed mill at Cannonsburg

A display at Fort Michilimackinac

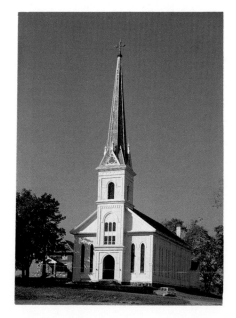

Drying the Fishing Nets

St. Patrick's Catholic Church in Parnell-
largest all wood church in Michigan

Old pine stump fencing

Paul Bunyan "Logging Wheel" at Hartwick Pines

Grindstone City in Michigan's Thumb area

Waishkey Bay Indian Burial Site in Bay Mills

AUTHOR'S NOTE

I hope this book will find a special place in your home where it can be enjoyed by all who see it. I have only shown you a small selection of the beauty and history that exists in Michigan. It's a special place, changing with each season. Learn all you can about it. If you live in Michigan, you can explore the state seven miles from home or venture with your family on a vacation that can go seven hundred miles. If you are traveling through Michigan, I'm sure you have only visited a fraction of the state. Plan to return and see more of what makes this state a unique wonderland.

Michigan is a special place. I am so lucky to have been raised here. I hope you share my love for and pride in Michigan.

About the Author

Anita McCollum was born in Saranac, Michigan in 1956. She is the daughter of Michigan photographer Hoyt Avery and spent her early years traveling to, visiting and learning about Michigan's two peninsulas.

Anita now resides with her husband and two children in Au Train, a small resort community, located in central Upper Michigan. Anita and her family, along with their two dogs and a tabby cat, enjoy all of what Michigan offers and have spent endless hours prowling through, snooping around and camping in Michigan. She is also active as a member of the local School Board, and through her involvement in the school system, began to see a need for a book on Michigan history for young readers.

"Come Explore Michigan the Beautiful" is the culmination of three year's research and two generations of photography, put together for readers of all ages.

Acknowledgments

A special thanks to Paul Kimball, Assistant Superintendent, Upper Peninsula Outreach Office, Michigan Department of Education, who has given me encouragement and guidance on this book. Also, I would like to express my appreciation to John Curry of the Michigan State Archives, the Michigan Travel Bureau, Jeheskel Shoshani of the Dept. of Biological Sciences at Wayne State University, Michigan Dept. of Natural Resources, Carol Avery, Chuck Landstrom, Barb Hase, Rep. Pat Gagliardi, Penny Hatt, Lori Howell, Karen Dubow, and my husband Mike.   *Thank you*

PLEASE RETURN TO:

Avery Color Studios
Star Route - Box 275
Au Train, Michigan 49806
Phone: (906) 892-8251
IN MICHIGAN
CALL TOLL FREE
1-800-722-9925

Your complete shipping address:

_____

_____

_____

_____

Fold, Staple, Affix Stamp and Mail

_____
_____
_____
_____

Avery COLOR STUDIOS
Star Route - Box 275
AuTrain, Michigan 49806